To Shelby – I will never forget you, sweet friend. ST

To my foster hounds, past, present and future. SM

For all the greyhounds dreaming of a loving family and a puppuccino. LP

"Susan Tanner's children's book about Salty, the rescued greyhound, is a lively, true story using a sing-song cadence to teach children about the love that all creatures crave and deserve, the importance of adoption, and the value of second chances. Organizations dedicated to rescuing racing greyhounds, like Gumtree Greys in Australia, give dogs like Salty a chance at a life full of love, puppuccinos, and snuggles, as Susan highlights in her carefree story. Susan and Salty bring children and adults together to laugh at Salty's candid photos and to bounce through the bubbly descriptions of Salty's life 'down under' in this heart-warming, happy-ending story."

Kelsey Gilmore-Futeral, Esq.
Secretary, Alliance of Therapy Dogs

Copyright © 2019 by Susan Tanner
ISBN: 978-1-7321-2920-7
Library of Congress Cataloging-in-Publication Data is available.

Scripture taken from the HOLY BIBLE, NEW INTERNATIONAL VERSION®. Copyright © 1973, 1978, 1984 by International Bible Society. Used by permission of Zondervan. All rights reserved.

Illustrations and design by Sophie McPike
www.sophiemcpike.com
on Instagram @sophiemcpike

Contributions by Lucy Percival
on Instagram @thesaltyhound

Published by Serendipity Crossing

SALT OF THE EARTH
A GREYHOUND LOVE STORY

Written by
Susan Tanner

Illustrated by
Sophie McPike

Contributions by
Lucy Percival

"You are the salt of the earth." Matthew 5:13

Salty is a rescue greyhound living with her humans, Lucy and Kieran, in Melbourne, Australia. Salty was a racing greyhound until Gumtree Greys gave her an opportunity for a new life.

Salty is truly the salt of the earth to her family. They cannot imagine life without her and the joy that she brings. Salty's favourite things are catching trains to go on adventures and having puppuccinos at local cafes.
Salty is known for her chattering teeth and natural overbite. Greyhounds often "chatter" their teeth when they are happy or excited.
Salty's Ma and Pa hope that through sharing her true story, more people will consider adopting a greyhound.

You can follow Salty's adventures on Instagram and other social media @thesaltyhound.

Gumtree Greys

Gumtree Greys is a volunteer rescue group dedicated to saving the lives of unwanted and/or retired racing greyhounds in Queensland and Victoria, Australia. We were established in Brisbane in 2013 to rescue and re-home the growing number of regionally-based greyhounds advertised on the onlinebuying and selling marketplace, Gumtree.

We are a supportive community of volunteers, foster carers and adopters, who have been brought together by the love of greyhounds and united by the belief that every greyhound is worth saving. As a not-for-profit, 100% volunteer-run organization which receives no funding from the racing industry, we rely completely on the generosity of our network and our donors to carry out our work. Everyone can help greyhounds find their new family. Please consider fostering or adopting a greyhound from Gumtree Greys or your local greyhound rescue group; you can also help by donating and volunteering.

Through our foster program, we take the time to learn about each greyhound to help them prepare for their new life. Our foster families provide greyhounds a safe home, and an opportunity to learn to be a pet before they meet their forever family.
We pride ourselves on matching greyhounds with the right home, making for happy hounds and happier families. Since our founding, Gumtree Greys has helped hundreds of greyhounds find their perfect family.

Follow Gumtree Greys on Facebook, Instagram, and YouTube to keep up-to-date with our community. To financially support the rescuing and rehoming of more greyhounds, visit our website gumtreegreys.com.au or our Etsy page.

A portion of the sale of this this book goes to Gumtree Greys to support their work.

There is a place Down Under that is full of wonder,
Where creatures roam without a care.

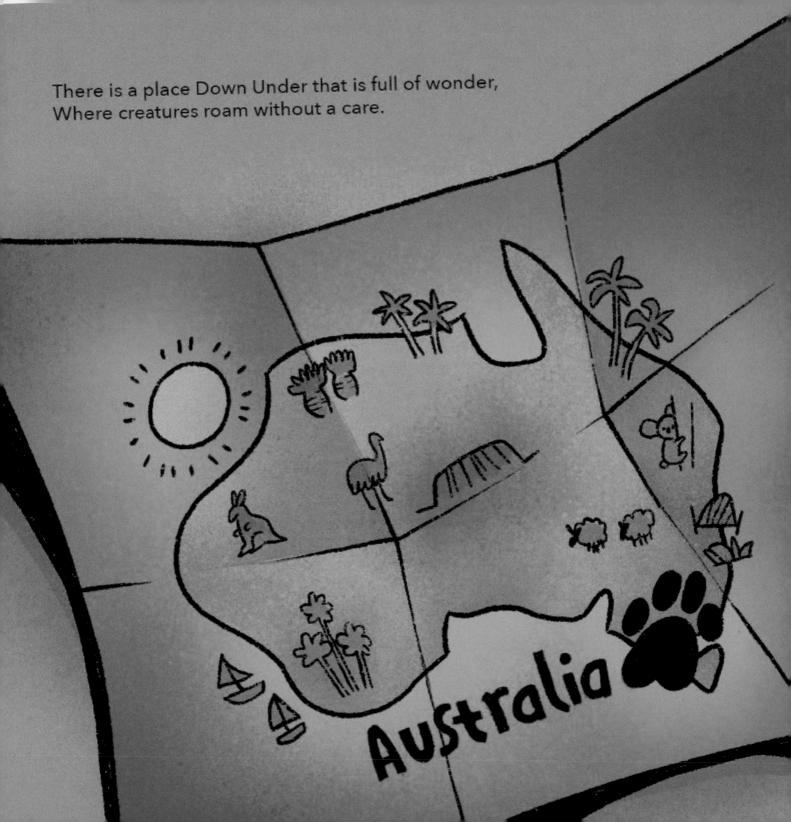

But the kangaroo, emu and cockatoo,
Cannot compare to one doggie so fair.

For in Melbourne town there lives a rescue hound,
World famous for her "toofers" that chatter.

Her friends call her Salty hound.
They know she is stardom bound,
With a smile that melts hearts,
Just look at 'er.

A racer in her younger days,
Salty knew life no other way,
'Til Gumtree Greys brought a change of fate.

When she heard Ma say, "G'day.
Won't you come home and play?
Life together will be so great!"

Salty's nose began to wiggle;
She gave her tail a lil' jiggle.
Her eyes twinkled with delight.

Ma tilted her ear... what did she hear?
It was the chatter of those pearly whites!

Ma and Pa shared a look, that was all that it took.
She laughed, "Let the adventures begin!"

Salty's days are now packed with train rides,
And ear pats,
And a chariot she takes for a spin.

There are puppaccinos in the morning,
Kisses without warning,
And snuggles with Cuddlepillar at nap.

There are walks with Salty's best friends,
Stretches that never end,
And relaxing manicures in Ma's lap.

The life of a princess,
An empress no less,
Is what Salty enjoys today.

And if you searched the earth over, from Dallas to Dover,
You will not find a more grateful Grey!

Susan Tanner lives in South Carolina, USA, with her husband, Greg, and their rescue dog, Sunshine. She truly hopes that Salty's story will encourage parents to consider adopting a greyhound when choosing a family pet so they can experience the loving qualities of this special breed.

Acknowledgements

I am eternally grateful to Lucy Percival and Gumtree Greys, as without their consent and support this story would not have come to fruition. It has also been a tremendous honor to work with Sophie McPike on this project, as her beautiful illustrations bring Salty's joyful spirit to life in such a delightful way.

I also wish to thank Kelsey Gilmore-Futeral for her insight into the animal rescue world, as well as special friends Rebekah, Donna, and Jenn.

I owe the most gratitude to my family, especially Audra, whose absolute confidence in me gave me the courage I needed to follow my dream.

Sophie McPike is a Melbourne, Australia based artist creating flower power, animal loving, whimsy and joyful illustrations and sculptures. Her work has a mixture of retro design and cheerful colour pallets with a dash of sweet self love reminders to make you smile.

Sophie grew up always surrounded by dogs; they were her best friends and she would spend hours playing with them all throughout her childhood. Sophie's compassion and love for dogs has resulted in many years of fostering greyhounds, rehabilitating them and showing them the love they all deserve. She will hopefully be a foster mum for many more years to come.

Dogs are better people than most people.
Be kind to your animal friends, you are their voice.

THE END

Made in the USA
Middletown, DE
18 December 2019